# THE POWER WITHIN:

## 9 Habits That Unlock Wealth, Fame, Power, and Success

By

F. A. Ebenezer

# Disclaimer

Copyright © by F. A. Ebenezer 2024. All rights reserved.

No part of this publication may be reproduced, stored in a retrieval system, or transmitted in any form or by any means, electronic, mechanical, photocopying, recording or otherwise, without the prior permission of the publisher.

# Table of Contents

Disclaimer ................................................................ 2
Table of Contents ................................................... 3
Introduction: The Path to Success ........................ 9
    Why Habits Shape Your Destiny ..................... 10
    The Relationship Between Mindset and Success ................................................................................ 11
Chapter 1: Embracing Failure – The Stepping Stone to Greatness .............................................. 14
    The Fear of Failure: Why It Holds You Back . 14
    How to Reframe Failures into Lessons ........... 16
    Stories of Successful People Who Failed First 18
Chapter 2: The Power of Vision – Crafting a Clear Future ......................................................... 22
    The Importance of a Clear Vision ................... 22
    Setting Meaningful Goals ............................... 24
    Visualizing Success: Techniques for Manifesting Your Dreams ................................................... 27

**Conclusion of Chapter 2** ................................ 30

Chapter 3: Lifelong Learning – The Secret to Continuous Growth ........................................... 32

   Why Learning Never Stops ........................... 32

   How to Cultivate a Growth Mindset ............... 34

   Practical Steps for Becoming a Lifelong Learner ........................................................................ 37

      Conclusion of Chapter 3 ............................ 40

Chapter 4: The Art of Listening – Connecting with People and Ideas .............................................. 42

   Why Listening is More Important Than Talking ........................................................................ 42

   How to Become an Effective Listener ........... 45

   The Power of Empathy and Understanding in Leadership ................................................... 48

   **Conclusion of Chapter 4** ............................ 50

Chapter 5: Proactivity – Taking Control of Your Future ............................................................. 51

The Difference Between Being Reactive and Proactive ........................................................ 51

How to Anticipate Opportunities and Challenges ................................................................................ 54

Strategies for Staying Ahead in Life and Business ................................................................................ 56

**Conclusion of Chapter 5** ............................ 59

Chapter 6: Valuing Relationships – Building a Network for Success ......................................... 61

Why Relationships Are the Foundation of Wealth and Power ...................................................... 61

Building Authentic Connections and Partnerships .................................................... 64

The Role of Mentorship and Giving Back ....... 67

Conclusion of Chapter 6 .............................. 69

Chapter 7: The Balance Factor – Mastering the Art of Life Harmony ............................................... 71

Why Balance Is Key to Sustainable Success ... 71

Strategies for Balancing Work, Family, and Personal Growth .................................................. 74

Avoiding Burnout While Pursuing Your Dreams .................................................................................... 77

Conclusion of Chapter 7 .............................. 80

Chapter 8: Patience – The Virtue that Guarantees Success ....................................................... 82

The Long Game: Why Patience is a Key to Wealth and Power .......................................... 82

How to Stay Focused and Committed Despite Delays ............................................................... 85

Celebrating Small Wins While Waiting for the Big Breakthrough .............................................. 88

**Conclusion of Chapter 8** ............................ 90

Chapter 9: Belief in Yourself: The Core of Unstoppable Success ........................................ 92

The Importance of Self-Confidence in Achieving Success ........................................................ 92

Techniques to Boost Your Self-Esteem and Inner Strength ............................................................. 95

How to Overcome Self-Doubt and Imposter Syndrome ................................................................ 98

   Conclusion of Chapter 9 ............................. 100

Chapter 10: Conclusion – Mastering the Habits of Success ....................................................... 102

   Putting It All Together: How These Habits Interconnect ................................................. 102

   Your Roadmap to Wealth, Fame, and Power 105

   Sustaining Success Over the Long Term ....... 108

     Conclusion of Chapter 10 ........................... 110

Chapter 11: Appendix – Resources for Personal Growth .......................................................... 112

   Recommended Books, Podcasts, and Courses ..................................................................... 112

   Journaling Prompts for Self-Reflection ......... 117

Tools for Tracking Progress on Your Journey ................................................................ 120
Conclusion of Chapter 11 ............................ 122

# Introduction: The Path to Success

Success, in its many forms—whether it be wealth, fame, power, or personal fulfillment—rarely happens by chance. It is the result of consistent, intentional actions over time. While talent and opportunity play a role, the real differentiator between those who merely dream of success and those who achieve it is their habits. Habits are the building blocks of life, shaping how we think, act, and respond to the world around us. As author John Dryden once said, "We first make our habits, and then our habits make us."

This book is about those habits—the nine fundamental practices that, when adopted, have the power to transform your life. It's about the mindset that propels ordinary people into extraordinary positions of influence and success. You may have heard of these habits individually, but together, they form a powerful blueprint for lasting success. Whether you are starting from a place of struggle or are already on a promising path, these habits will act as a guide, helping you unlock the potential within you.

## Why Habits Shape Your Destiny

Our lives are a reflection of the small, daily decisions we make. Habits, by their very nature, are repetitive actions—things we do without even thinking. Over time, they accumulate, steering our lives in a particular direction. If our habits are positive and growth-oriented, they lead us toward success. If they are negative or destructive, they hold us back, often without us even realizing it.

Imagine the trajectory of two people. One spends an hour every morning reading and learning something new. The other spends that same hour scrolling through social media. In one day, the difference is subtle. But in a year, the reader will have amassed an incredible wealth of knowledge, while the other will have little to show for their time. This is the power of habits—tiny actions that, compounded over time, shape our future.

Many people mistakenly believe that success is about making one big, bold move at the right time. In reality, it's the consistent application of small, positive habits that creates the foundation for long-term achievement.

Habits dictate how we approach challenges, how we seize opportunities, and how we navigate the inevitable setbacks along the way. When you are disciplined in your habits, you gain control over your destiny.

## The Relationship Between Mindset and Success

At the heart of every habit is your mindset—the way you perceive yourself and the world around you. It's no coincidence that people who achieve remarkable success often share similar mental attitudes. They are resilient in the face of failure, optimistic about the future, and committed to continuous improvement.

Your mindset acts as the operating system that drives your habits. A growth mindset, as described by psychologist Carol Dweck, is the belief that abilities and intelligence can be developed through effort and learning. People with a growth mindset embrace challenges, persevere through difficulties, and view failure as a learning experience.

In contrast, a fixed mindset leads to avoidance of challenges, fear of failure, and a tendency to give up easily.

The nine habits you'll learn about in this book are deeply intertwined with the concept of mindset. For example, being unafraid of failure is impossible without a growth mindset. A person who believes they can grow from their mistakes will take risks, while someone with a fixed mindset will avoid anything that might expose them to failure. Similarly, believing in yourself is a mindset that directly impacts how you approach challenges and opportunities.

This book will show you how to align your mindset with the habits that lead to success. It will help you shift your thinking, so you can cultivate the habits necessary to unlock your potential. As you read, you'll begin to understand that success isn't just about what you do—it's about how you think, and how your thinking fuels the actions that shape your destiny.

In the chapters ahead, you'll discover the habits that have the power to change everything.

They are not quick fixes or shortcuts, but time-tested principles that have propelled many individuals from obscurity to greatness. Whether you are striving for financial success, personal fulfillment, or influence, these habits, when adopted and practiced consistently, will help you achieve your goals.

Welcome to the journey of mastering the habits of success. It starts here—with a mindset focused on growth, and habits that will drive you toward the life you've always envisioned.

# Chapter 1: Embracing Failure – The Stepping Stone to Greatness

Failure is often seen as the end of the road—a barrier that blocks us from reaching our goals. Yet, for those who have truly achieved greatness, failure is not an obstacle but a critical stepping stone. Success and failure are not opposites; they are deeply intertwined, and failure is often the catalyst that propels us toward success. In this chapter, we will explore why fear of failure holds so many people back, how you can reframe your perspective to see failure as a teacher, and look at the inspiring stories of people who turned failure into triumph.

## The Fear of Failure: Why It Holds You Back

Fear of failure is a powerful force that paralyzes many. It's rooted in a deep concern about what failure says about us—whether it marks us as incompetent, unworthy, or inadequate. This fear can prevent people from taking risks, trying new things, or even pursuing their dreams.

The irony, of course, is that the fear of failure is often what leads to stagnation and, ultimately, failure itself.

Why does this fear have such a strong grip on us? For one, society tends to celebrate success and shun failure. From a young age, we are conditioned to avoid mistakes at all costs, and we internalize the idea that failure is something to be ashamed of. This mindset creates an aversion to risk, and we start avoiding any situation where failure might be a possibility. But when we do this, we also avoid growth.

In truth, failure is an inevitable part of life. Anyone who sets out to achieve something meaningful will face setbacks. The key is not to avoid failure but to embrace it as part of the journey. Instead of seeing failure as a reflection of your worth, see it as feedback—an opportunity to learn, adapt, and improve. When you stop fearing failure, you unlock your potential to take bold action, innovate, and push past limits that once seemed impossible.

## How to Reframe Failures into Lessons

If you're going to embrace failure as a stepping stone to greatness, the first step is to change your mindset around it. Failure doesn't mean the end; it means that you've found one way that doesn't work, and now you're closer to finding a way that does. The people who succeed aren't the ones who never fail—they are the ones who fail, learn, and keep going.

Here are a few ways to reframe failure into valuable lessons:

1. **See Failure as Feedback**: Every failure is telling you something—whether it's about your approach, your strategy, or your mindset. Instead of dwelling on the emotional sting of failure, ask yourself: *What can I learn from this? What can I do differently next time?* By focusing on the lesson rather than the loss, you turn failure into a stepping stone for improvement.
2. **Detach Your Ego from the Outcome**: One of the reasons failure feels so painful is because we tie it to our sense of self-worth.

If you can detach your identity from the outcome, failure loses much of its sting. You are not your failures. Failing at a task doesn't make you a failure as a person—it just means the method you used didn't work. Separate the process from your self-worth, and it becomes much easier to try again.

3. **Celebrate the Effort, Not Just the Outcome**:
   It's easy to focus only on results, but the effort you put in matters just as much. Even if you don't achieve the desired outcome, acknowledge the courage it took to try, the lessons learned along the way, and the resilience you gained from facing failure. Each attempt builds you into someone stronger and more capable.
4. **Fail Fast, Fail Often**:
   In the world of startups and innovation, there's a popular saying: *Fail fast, fail often*. This means embracing failure as an inevitable part of progress and not being afraid to experiment. The faster you fail, the faster you learn what doesn't work, which leads you to what does work more quickly.

By reframing failure in these ways, you can turn what once seemed like a dead-end into a vital part of your growth process. The sooner you make peace with failure, the sooner you can start using it to your advantage.

## Stories of Successful People Who Failed First

Failure is a common thread in the stories of many successful people. Their achievements are often celebrated, but what's less discussed is the series of failures that preceded their breakthroughs. Here are some examples of individuals who turned failure into greatness:

1. **Thomas Edison**: Thomas Edison is famous for inventing the electric lightbulb, but the road to his success was paved with thousands of failed experiments. When asked about his failures, Edison reportedly said, *"I have not failed. I've just found 10,000 ways that won't work."*

His persistence paid off, and today, his invention is one of the most significant in modern history.

2. **J.K. Rowling**:
Before J.K. Rowling became one of the most successful authors in the world with her *Harry Potter* series, she faced multiple rejections from publishers. She was a single mother living on welfare, struggling to make ends meet. Her manuscript was rejected by 12 different publishers before finally being accepted. Rowling's story is a powerful reminder that failure and rejection are not final—they are simply part of the process.

3. **Steve Jobs**:
Steve Jobs is hailed as one of the greatest visionaries of our time, but his journey to success was far from smooth. In 1985, Jobs was fired from Apple, the very company he had co-founded. Devastated but determined, he didn't let this failure define him.

Instead, he went on to create another successful company, NeXT, and later returned to Apple, transforming it into the global powerhouse it is today. Jobs' story exemplifies how failure can be the foundation for an even greater comeback.

4. **Oprah Winfrey**: Oprah Winfrey's rise to fame is a testament to resilience. Early in her career, she was fired from her job as a television news anchor because she was told she was "unfit for TV." Instead of giving up, Oprah pursued her passion and eventually became one of the most influential media moguls in the world. Her ability to learn from failure and continue pursuing her vision led to immense success.

These stories illustrate a universal truth: failure is not the end—it is merely a step along the path to greatness. The common thread among all these individuals is that they didn't let failure stop them. Instead, they used it as fuel to keep going, to innovate, and to eventually achieve extraordinary success.

**Conclusion of Chapter 1**
Embracing failure is not just about tolerating setbacks; it's about seeing failure as an integral part of the journey to success. Every failure brings you one step closer to your goal, as long as you are willing to learn from it. When you stop fearing failure, you start taking the bold actions necessary to achieve greatness. By reframing failure and studying the stories of those who failed first, you'll see that every setback is an opportunity in disguise.

# Chapter 2: The Power of Vision – Crafting a Clear Future

Vision is the blueprint for your future, the mental picture of where you want to go and what you want to achieve. Without a clear vision, it's easy to drift through life, reacting to circumstances rather than shaping them. Successful people, however, are often characterized by their strong sense of vision—they know where they're headed, and this clarity guides their decisions, actions, and strategies. This chapter explores the importance of having a clear vision, how to set meaningful goals, and techniques for visualizing success to bring your dreams to life.

## The Importance of a Clear Vision

Having a clear vision is like having a map in unfamiliar territory. It provides direction, purpose, and motivation. Without it, you may work hard, but your efforts could be scattered, leading to frustration and a lack of meaningful progress.

A clear vision anchors you, helping you stay focused even when challenges arise.

Vision is more than just wishful thinking; it's a concrete, detailed mental image of what you want to achieve. When your vision is clear, you're more likely to recognize opportunities and make decisions that align with your desired future. It becomes easier to stay motivated because you can see the end result, even when the present moment is difficult.

People without a vision tend to live in reaction to the world around them, allowing external circumstances to dictate their choices. They chase short-term wins, often at the expense of long-term fulfillment. On the other hand, people with a clear vision act with intention. They know that every action they take today is moving them closer to their ultimate goal. This long-term perspective gives them a sense of purpose and the resilience to navigate setbacks.

Having a clear vision also inspires others.

Visionary leaders, entrepreneurs, and innovators are often able to rally others around them because their clarity of purpose is contagious. When you are clear about your own vision, it becomes easier to communicate it to others and attract support, partnerships, and opportunities that align with your goals.

## Setting Meaningful Goals

Once you have a clear vision, the next step is setting meaningful goals that will help you achieve it. Your vision is the destination, but your goals are the milestones that will get you there. Without specific goals, your vision remains a dream. Goals break down your vision into actionable, measurable steps, making it easier to track progress and stay on course.

Here are some key principles for setting meaningful goals:

1. **Make Your Goals Specific and Measurable**:

Vague goals like "I want to be successful" or "I want to make more money" won't get you very far. Instead, be specific about what success looks like to you. For example, if your vision is to become a successful entrepreneur, a specific goal might be "Start my own online business within six months and generate $50,000 in revenue within the first year." Specific and measurable goals allow you to track your progress and know when you've reached a milestone.

2. **Set Realistic but Ambitious Goals**: Your goals should stretch you, but they shouldn't be so unrealistic that they feel impossible. Striking the right balance between ambition and realism is crucial for maintaining motivation. Goals that are too easy won't push you to grow, while goals that seem unattainable can lead to frustration and burnout.
3. **Break Your Goals Down into Smaller Steps**:
Large goals can feel overwhelming, so it's important to break them down into smaller, manageable steps.

For example, if your goal is to write a book, you might break it down into smaller tasks such as drafting an outline, writing a chapter each week, and editing the manuscript. Each small achievement builds momentum and keeps you moving toward your larger vision.

4. **Set Deadlines**: A goal without a deadline is just a wish. Setting a timeline for each goal creates a sense of urgency and helps you stay accountable. Deadlines also allow you to measure your progress and make adjustments if necessary. If you miss a deadline, don't give up—just reassess and set a new one.
5. **Review and Adjust Your Goals Regularly**: Life is dynamic, and your goals may need to evolve as circumstances change. Regularly reviewing your goals ensures that they remain aligned with your vision and allows you to make adjustments when needed. This flexibility keeps you adaptable and responsive, without losing sight of your ultimate destination.

By setting meaningful goals that align with your vision, you create a roadmap for success. Every goal achieved brings you one step closer to turning your vision into reality.

## Visualizing Success: Techniques for Manifesting Your Dreams

Visualization is a powerful mental practice that allows you to see your future success before it happens. When you visualize, you mentally rehearse your desired outcomes, creating a vivid picture of what it feels like to achieve your goals. This technique helps align your thoughts, emotions, and actions with your vision, making it more likely that you'll take the steps needed to turn it into reality.

Scientific research supports the effectiveness of visualization. Athletes, entrepreneurs, and high achievers across many fields use visualization to mentally prepare for success.

The brain can't always distinguish between real experiences and vividly imagined ones, which means that visualizing success can help you develop the confidence and focus necessary to achieve it.

Here are some visualization techniques that can help you manifest your dreams:

1. **Create a Detailed Mental Picture**: Visualization works best when you create a detailed and vivid mental image of your desired outcome. Imagine not only what success looks like but also what it feels like. What are the sights, sounds, and emotions associated with reaching your goals? For example, if your vision is to become a successful public speaker, visualize yourself standing confidently in front of a large audience, delivering your message with clarity and passion. Feel the energy of the crowd, hear the applause, and experience the pride of having made an impact.
2. **Use Visualization Daily**: Visualization is most effective when practiced consistently.

Set aside a few minutes each day to close your eyes and mentally rehearse your future success. Whether it's first thing in the morning or right before bed, daily visualization helps keep your vision at the forefront of your mind and reinforces your commitment to achieving it.

3. **Combine Visualization with Affirmations**: Positive affirmations are powerful statements that reinforce your belief in your ability to succeed. Combining visualization with affirmations can amplify their impact. For example, while visualizing your success, repeat affirmations like "I am capable of achieving my goals" or "I am on the path to greatness." These affirmations help reprogram your subconscious mind, replacing self-doubt with confidence and determination.
4. **Visualize the Process, Not Just the Outcome**:
While it's important to visualize the end result, it's equally important to visualize the steps you'll need to take to get there.

Mentally rehearse the challenges you may face and how you'll overcome them. By visualizing both the process and the outcome, you prepare yourself for the hard work and persistence required to achieve your vision.

5. **Use Vision Boards for Inspiration**: A vision board is a visual representation of your goals and dreams.It's a physical or digital collage of images, quotes, and words that represent the life you want to create. Vision boards serve as a constant reminder of your aspirations and can help you stay focused on your goals. Place your vision board somewhere you'll see it daily, so it inspires you to take action toward your dreams.

**Conclusion of Chapter 2**

Vision is the foundation of success. It gives you a clear sense of direction and purpose, allowing you to set meaningful goals that guide your actions.

When combined with the power of visualization, your vision becomes more than just an idea—it becomes a reality in the making. The clearer your vision, the more likely you are to recognize opportunities, overcome challenges, and stay motivated on your journey to success.

By mastering the art of vision, goal-setting, and visualization, you equip yourself with the tools to craft a future that aligns with your deepest aspirations. This is the power of vision: the ability to see the future you want and to take the steps necessary to bring it into existence.

# Chapter 3: Lifelong Learning – The Secret to Continuous Growth

In a world that's constantly evolving, staying stagnant is not an option. Those who achieve enduring success understand that learning is a lifelong journey, not a destination. Lifelong learning is the secret to continuous growth and personal development, allowing you to stay ahead in your field, adapt to changes, and unlock new opportunities. This chapter delves into the importance of never-ending learning, how to cultivate a growth mindset, and practical steps you can take to become a lifelong learner.

## Why Learning Never Stops

The world we live in is in a state of constant flux. Technology advances rapidly, industries change, and new ideas emerge all the time. In this dynamic environment, what worked yesterday may not work tomorrow.

The most successful people recognize that their knowledge and skills must evolve to stay relevant and competitive. They are constantly learning, adapting, and improving.

Lifelong learning goes beyond formal education. It's about being curious, seeking out new information, and challenging yourself to grow. It keeps your mind sharp, enhances creativity, and helps you remain open to new opportunities. When you stop learning, you risk falling behind. But when you embrace the mindset that learning never stops, you continually position yourself for growth.

Lifelong learning also has profound benefits for your personal life. It improves your problem-solving abilities, enhances critical thinking, and boosts your confidence. The more you know, the more you can contribute to conversations, projects, and relationships. Whether you're learning a new skill, exploring a different subject, or deepening your expertise in your current field, every bit of knowledge you acquire helps you grow as a person.

# How to Cultivate a Growth Mindset

The foundation of lifelong learning is a growth mindset—the belief that your abilities and intelligence can be developed through effort, persistence, and learning. This concept, popularized by psychologist Carol Dweck, contrasts with a fixed mindset, where people believe their talents and intelligence are static traits.

With a growth mindset, you see challenges as opportunities to learn rather than as threats to your abilities. You understand that failure is part of the learning process, not a reflection of your worth. This mindset encourages you to seek out new experiences, push your limits, and view setbacks as valuable lessons.

Here are key ways to cultivate a growth mindset:

1. **Embrace Challenges**: People with a growth mindset thrive on challenges because they know that challenges help them grow.

Instead of shying away from difficult tasks, see them as opportunities to stretch your abilities. By tackling challenges head-on, you build resilience and confidence, which fuel your personal and professional growth.

2. **Learn from Criticism**: Feedback is a powerful tool for growth, but only if you are willing to listen and learn from it. Instead of taking criticism personally, view it as valuable information that can help you improve. Ask yourself: *What can I learn from this feedback? How can I use it to get better?* This approach not only helps you develop but also strengthens your relationships with those who offer constructive criticism.
3. **Value Effort Over Talent**: A growth mindset prioritizes effort and persistence over innate talent. Rather than believing you either "have it" or you don't, recognize that mastery comes through hard work, dedication, and continuous learning.

Celebrate the process of learning, not just the outcome. The more effort you put into learning, the more progress you'll see.

4. **Reframe Setbacks as Learning Opportunities**:
   Every setback is a chance to learn something new. When things don't go as planned, don't get discouraged. Instead, ask yourself what lessons you can take away from the experience. Whether it's a failed project or a personal mistake, each setback offers insights that can help you grow stronger and more capable.

5. **Surround Yourself with Growth-Oriented People**:
   Your environment plays a huge role in shaping your mindset. Surround yourself with people who are also committed to learning and growth. Engage in discussions, share knowledge, and seek inspiration from those who value continuous improvement. This kind of environment reinforces the growth mindset and keeps you motivated to keep learning.

# Practical Steps for Becoming a Lifelong Learner

Becoming a lifelong learner is a conscious choice that requires ongoing effort and commitment. Fortunately, there are many practical ways to integrate continuous learning into your life, no matter your schedule or interests. Here are some steps to help you embrace lifelong learning:

1. **Read Regularly**: One of the simplest and most effective ways to continue learning is by reading. Books, articles, and research papers are treasure troves of knowledge that can expand your understanding of any topic. Make reading a habit by setting aside time each day to read something new. Whether it's a book on personal development, a business publication, or a novel, reading stimulates your mind and exposes you to new ideas.
2. **Take Online Courses**: The internet has made it easier than ever to learn new skills.

Platforms like Coursera, Udemy, and LinkedIn Learning offer thousands of courses on virtually every topic. Whether you want to learn coding, marketing, photography, or leadership, there's an online course for it. Set a goal to complete one or two courses each year to keep your skills fresh and up-to-date.

3. **Attend Workshops and Seminars**: In-person or virtual workshops and seminars offer opportunities to learn from experts and network with like-minded individuals. These events often provide hands-on learning experiences and insights that you can't get from books alone. Look for industry conferences, webinars, or local workshops that align with your interests and professional goals.
4. **Develop a New Skill**: Challenge yourself to learn a new skill that's outside of your current expertise.

Whether it's learning a new language, mastering a musical instrument, or picking up a technical skill like coding or graphic design, stepping out of your comfort zone forces your brain to grow. Plus, acquiring new skills opens doors to new hobbies, opportunities, and relationships.

5. **Practice Self-Reflection**: Reflection is an important part of the learning process. Take time to think about what you've learned, how you've grown, and what you still want to achieve. Journaling, meditating, or simply taking a few minutes each day to reflect on your experiences helps you internalize lessons and stay focused on growth.
6. **Engage in Meaningful Conversations**: Conversations with others can be a rich source of learning. Engage with people from different backgrounds, industries, and perspectives. Ask questions, listen carefully, and share your own experiences.

These exchanges not only broaden your understanding but also allow you to apply what you've learned in practical, real-world situations.

7. **Experiment and Innovate**: Lifelong learners aren't afraid to experiment. Don't be afraid to try new things, even if they don't always lead to immediate success. Innovation comes from a willingness to explore uncharted territory. Whether it's in your personal life or professional career, taking risks and experimenting with new ideas keeps you learning and growing.

**Conclusion of Chapter 3**

Lifelong learning is not a luxury; it's a necessity for anyone who wants to stay relevant, successful, and fulfilled in today's fast-paced world. The commitment to continuous learning fuels personal and professional growth, allowing you to adapt to change and seize new opportunities.

Cultivating a growth mindset is the key to embracing lifelong learning, as it encourages you to view challenges, effort, and feedback as vital components of your development.

By incorporating practical steps—such as reading regularly, taking online courses, and engaging in meaningful conversations—you can make learning an integral part of your life. Lifelong learners understand that knowledge is infinite, and the pursuit of learning is a journey without an end. The more you learn, the more you grow, and the more equipped you become to achieve greatness in every area of life.

# Chapter 4: The Art of Listening – Connecting with People and Ideas

Listening is often underestimated in a world where everyone wants to be heard. We live in an era where talking, sharing opinions, and expressing ourselves have become dominant forms of communication. Yet, the most successful and impactful individuals understand that listening—truly listening—is one of the most powerful tools for building strong relationships, understanding new ideas, and becoming a better leader.

This chapter explores why listening is more important than talking, how you can develop the skill of effective listening, and how empathy and understanding play a crucial role in leadership and success.

## Why Listening is More Important Than Talking

We've all heard the saying, "You have two ears and one mouth for a reason."

While it might seem cliché, it holds deep wisdom. Listening is often more valuable than talking because it allows you to gain insight, gather information, and build stronger connections with others. When you listen, you give yourself the opportunity to learn and understand. This is something that talking alone cannot achieve.

Talking tends to focus on expressing our own ideas, opinions, and needs. Listening, on the other hand, shifts the focus from ourselves to others. When you listen, you learn what others think, feel, and need. You gain perspective that can shape your decisions and actions. In fact, many of life's greatest opportunities come not from what we say, but from what we hear.

Here are a few reasons why listening is more important than talking:

1. **Listening Builds Trust and Rapport**: People trust those who listen to them. When someone feels heard, they feel valued, respected, and understood. This fosters a deeper connection and strengthens relationships.

Whether in personal or professional settings, listening is the foundation for building trust, which is essential for collaboration and success.

2. **Listening Opens the Door to New Ideas**: By actively listening to others, you expose yourself to new ideas and perspectives. These insights can expand your own understanding of the world and spark creativity. Many breakthrough innovations come from listening to the needs and ideas of others, rather than imposing your own thoughts.
3. **Listening Helps You Solve Problems**: Effective problem-solving often requires a deep understanding of the issue at hand, which can only be achieved through careful listening. When you truly listen to people's concerns or challenges, you gather the information needed to find solutions that address the root of the problem.
4. **Listening Shows Respect**: Talking over others or not paying attention while someone speaks is a sign of disrespect.

On the contrary, when you give someone your full attention, it shows that you value their thoughts and contributions. This can significantly enhance relationships, especially in leadership roles.

## How to Become an Effective Listener

Listening may seem like a simple skill, but it requires intention and practice to do it well. Effective listening is about more than just hearing words—it's about understanding the message behind those words, reading between the lines, and responding thoughtfully. Becoming an effective listener can transform your relationships, leadership abilities, and overall success.

Here are some practical steps to become an effective listener:

1. **Be Present and Focused**: One of the key components of effective listening is being fully present in the moment. This means putting away distractions—like your phone or other devices—and giving your full attention to the person speaking.

When you're distracted, it's impossible to truly listen. Focus on the speaker's words, tone, and body language to gain a deeper understanding of their message.

2. **Practice Active Listening**: Active listening involves engaging with the speaker to show that you are not only hearing them but also processing what they're saying. You can do this by nodding, asking clarifying questions, and summarizing what the speaker has said to ensure you understand. For example, phrases like "What I'm hearing is…" or "It sounds like you're saying…" show that you're fully engaged in the conversation.
3. **Avoid Interrupting**: One of the most common barriers to effective listening is interrupting. When you interrupt someone, it's often because you're more focused on what you want to say next than on what the speaker is saying. Resist the urge to jump in with your own thoughts until the speaker has finished.

Not only does this allow for better understanding, but it also shows respect for the speaker's contribution.

4. **Pay Attention to Non-Verbal Cues**: Communication is about more than words. Body language, facial expressions, and tone of voice can convey emotions and messages that words alone cannot. As you listen, pay attention to these non-verbal cues. They often provide valuable context to what the speaker is saying and can help you grasp the full meaning behind their words.
5. **Ask Thoughtful Questions**: Asking questions shows that you're engaged and interested in what the speaker is saying. It also gives you the chance to deepen your understanding of the topic. Instead of asking simple yes or no questions, try asking open-ended questions that encourage the speaker to elaborate. For example, "Can you tell me more about that?" or "How did that make you feel?" can lead to richer conversations and insights.

# The Power of Empathy and Understanding in Leadership

One of the most important aspects of being a great listener—especially in leadership—is empathy. Empathy is the ability to understand and share the feelings of another person. When leaders listen with empathy, they build trust, loyalty, and respect among their team members. They also gain valuable insight into the challenges, motivations, and needs of their team, which can inform better decision-making.

Here's how empathy and understanding can elevate leadership:

1. **Building Stronger Connections**: Empathetic leaders listen not just to the words but to the emotions behind those words. They take the time to understand how their team members are feeling and what drives them. This creates a deeper bond and sense of loyalty between the leader and their team, fostering a more collaborative and supportive work environment.

2. **Improving Decision-Making**: Leaders who listen empathetically are better equipped to make informed decisions. By understanding the perspectives and concerns of their team members, they can address problems more effectively and create solutions that work for everyone. Empathy allows leaders to see the bigger picture and avoid making decisions that could negatively impact the team or organization.
3. **Resolving Conflicts**: Conflict is inevitable in any team, but empathetic leaders are better at resolving it. When a leader listens with empathy, they can get to the root of the issue and address the underlying emotions that may be fueling the conflict. By understanding both sides of a disagreement, leaders can mediate and find solutions that satisfy all parties involved.
4. **Inspiring Loyalty and Trust**: Leaders who listen and demonstrate understanding inspire loyalty in their followers. People are more likely to trust and support a leader who takes the time to listen to their concerns and ideas.

This trust leads to higher morale, increased productivity, and a stronger sense of unity within the team.

**Conclusion of Chapter 4**

Listening is more than just a passive act; it is an art form that can transform your relationships, leadership, and personal success. While many people focus on talking to get their point across, those who master the art of listening will connect more deeply with others, gain valuable insights, and build lasting trust.

By practicing active listening, avoiding interruptions, paying attention to non-verbal cues, and asking thoughtful questions, you can become a more effective listener. Coupled with empathy, listening can elevate your leadership and make you a more compassionate, respected, and successful individual. The art of listening is a lifelong skill that will not only help you understand others better but will also open doors to new opportunities, ideas, and growth.

# Chapter 5: Proactivity – Taking Control of Your Future

In the journey toward success, being proactive is a cornerstone of achieving your goals and shaping your destiny. Proactivity involves taking control of your actions and decisions rather than merely reacting to events as they happen. It's about anticipating opportunities and challenges, making strategic choices, and taking deliberate steps toward your objectives. This chapter explores the difference between being reactive and proactive, how to anticipate and navigate opportunities and challenges, and strategies for staying ahead in both life and business.

## The Difference Between Being Reactive and Proactive

Understanding the difference between being reactive and proactive is essential for personal and professional growth. Reactive individuals respond to situations after they occur, often driven by circumstances or external pressures.

They may feel like they're always putting out fires, dealing with problems as they arise, and often find themselves caught off guard by unforeseen challenges.

On the other hand, proactive individuals take initiative and plan ahead. They anticipate potential issues and opportunities, prepare for them in advance, and make informed decisions that align with their long-term goals. Proactivity is about taking control of your actions and outcomes, rather than letting circumstances dictate your path.

Here's a deeper look at the key differences between reactive and proactive behaviors:

1. **Response to Situations**:
    - **Reactive**: Reacts to problems as they arise, often with a sense of urgency and stress. Their actions are often driven by immediate needs and external factors.
    - **Proactive**: Anticipates potential issues and plans accordingly. They take preemptive actions to address challenges before they become problems.

2. **Control Over Outcomes**:
   - **Reactive**: Feels like they have limited control over outcomes, as they are constantly responding to situations rather than directing their own path.
   - **Proactive**: Takes ownership of their future and makes deliberate choices that shape their desired outcomes.
3. **Mindset**:
   - **Reactive**: Has a mindset focused on managing crises and dealing with what comes their way.
   - **Proactive**: Adopts a mindset of planning, foresight, and strategic action.
4. **Focus**:
   - **Reactive**: Often focuses on solving problems and putting out fires, which can lead to short-term thinking and a lack of long-term vision.
   - **Proactive**: Focuses on long-term goals and strategies, ensuring that their actions align with their overall objectives.

# How to Anticipate Opportunities and Challenges

Being proactive requires the ability to anticipate and prepare for both opportunities and challenges. This foresight allows you to stay ahead of the curve, making informed decisions and positioning yourself for success. Here are some strategies for anticipating opportunities and challenges:

1. **Conduct Regular SWOT Analyses**: SWOT (Strengths, Weaknesses, Opportunities, Threats) analysis is a valuable tool for understanding your position and planning strategically. By regularly assessing your strengths and weaknesses and identifying potential opportunities and threats, you can develop strategies to leverage your advantages and address potential issues.
2. **Stay Informed and Curious**: Keeping up with industry trends, market changes, and emerging technologies is crucial for identifying opportunities.

Subscribe to relevant publications, attend industry events, and engage with thought leaders to stay informed. Curiosity about the world around you will help you spot trends and opportunities that others might overlook.

3. **Network and Build Relationships**: Building a strong network of professional and personal connections can provide valuable insights and open doors to new opportunities. Engage with people in your industry, seek mentorship, and participate in relevant communities. Your network can offer advice, share information, and provide support as you navigate your path.
4. **Set Clear Goals and Monitor Progress**: Establishing clear goals helps you focus on what you want to achieve and provides a framework for anticipating opportunities and challenges. Regularly review your goals and progress, and adjust your plans as needed. This proactive approach allows you to stay on track and adapt to changes along the way.
5. **Develop Contingency Plans**:

Preparing for potential challenges involves creating contingency plans for various scenarios. Consider what could go wrong and how you would respond. Having backup plans in place helps you manage risks and maintain control even when unexpected issues arise.

6. **Use Data and Analytics**: Leverage data and analytics to make informed decisions and anticipate future trends. Analyzing data related to your industry, market, or personal performance can provide insights that help you identify opportunities and challenges before they become apparent.

## Strategies for Staying Ahead in Life and Business

To remain proactive and stay ahead in life and business, it's essential to adopt strategies that support long-term success and continuous improvement. Here are some effective strategies to help you stay ahead:

1. **Develop a Strategic Plan**: A strategic plan outlines your long-term goals and the steps needed to achieve them. It includes setting objectives, identifying key actions, and establishing timelines. Regularly review and update your plan to reflect changes in your goals, environment, and opportunities.
2. **Prioritize Time Management**: Effective time management is crucial for staying proactive. Use tools like calendars, to-do lists, and time-tracking apps to organize your tasks and priorities. Allocate time for planning, strategic thinking, and proactive activities, ensuring that you stay focused on your long-term goals.
3. **Invest in Personal Development**: Continuously improving your skills and knowledge is essential for staying ahead. Invest in personal development through training, education, and self-improvement activities. This ongoing learning helps you adapt to changes and remain competitive in your field.

4. **Foster Innovation and Creativity**: Encourage innovation and creativity in your approach to problem-solving and decision-making. Look for new ways to improve processes, develop products, or approach challenges. Being innovative helps you stay ahead of the competition and seize new opportunities.
5. **Embrace Change and Adaptability**: Change is a constant in both life and business. Embrace change with a positive attitude and be willing to adapt your strategies and plans as needed. Flexibility and adaptability are key components of proactive behavior, allowing you to navigate uncertainty and capitalize on new opportunities.
6. **Monitor and Evaluate Performance**: Regularly assess your performance and progress toward your goals. Use performance metrics and feedback to evaluate what's working and what needs improvement. This proactive evaluation allows you to make adjustments and stay aligned with your objectives.

7. **Cultivate a Problem-Solving Mindset**: Approach challenges with a problem-solving mindset. Instead of being discouraged by obstacles, view them as opportunities to find solutions and improve. Developing a proactive approach to problem-solving helps you address issues effectively and maintain momentum toward your goals.

## Conclusion of Chapter 5

Proactivity is a powerful trait that enables you to take control of your future and shape your success. By understanding the difference between being reactive and proactive, and by employing strategies to anticipate opportunities and challenges, you position yourself to achieve your goals and navigate the complexities of life and business effectively.

Embracing a proactive mindset involves taking deliberate actions, planning for the future, and continuously seeking improvement. It requires staying informed, building strong relationships, and being adaptable in the face of change.

When you harness the power of proactivity, you gain the ability to control your destiny, overcome obstacles, and create the future you envision.

# Chapter 6: Valuing Relationships – Building a Network for Success

In the pursuit of wealth, power, and success, relationships are often the foundation upon which everything else is built. Your network—the people you interact with, learn from, and support—plays a significant role in shaping your personal and professional journey. Building strong, authentic relationships helps you gain access to opportunities, resources, and knowledge that would otherwise be out of reach. This chapter focuses on why relationships are crucial to success, how to build meaningful connections, and the importance of mentorship and giving back.

## Why Relationships Are the Foundation of Wealth and Power

No one achieves great success alone. Behind every successful individual is a network of people who provide support, guidance, resources, and opportunities.

Relationships are the cornerstone of wealth and power because they help you access valuable information, open doors to new opportunities, and provide the emotional and practical support needed to navigate challenges.

Here are some key reasons why relationships form the foundation of success:

1. **Access to Opportunities**: Many opportunities in life—whether it's a job, a business venture, or an investment—come through connections. Knowing the right people can open doors that would otherwise remain closed. Your network connects you to potential partners, clients, and mentors who can help you grow and achieve your goals.
2. **Leveraging Knowledge and Expertise**: Building relationships with knowledgeable and experienced individuals allows you to learn from their expertise.

Whether it's gaining insights into an industry, learning new skills, or seeking advice, the people around you provide valuable guidance that accelerates your growth.

3. **Emotional Support and Encouragement**: Success is not always a linear path, and the road can be filled with challenges and setbacks. Having strong relationships offers emotional support during tough times. A trusted friend, partner, or mentor can provide encouragement, motivation, and a fresh perspective when you need it most.
4. **Expanding Your Influence**: Wealth and power often come from influence—being able to impact others and make decisions that shape outcomes. The broader your network, the more influence you can exert in your personal and professional circles. Relationships help you expand your reach and create alliances that strengthen your position.
5. **Collaboration and Synergy**: Collaboration is at the heart of success in business and life.

By building a network of like-minded individuals, you can collaborate on projects, share resources, and combine talents to achieve greater results. Synergy arises when people work together, creating outcomes that are greater than the sum of their individual efforts.

## Building Authentic Connections and Partnerships

Building relationships goes beyond simply collecting business cards or adding contacts on social media. Meaningful, authentic connections are based on trust, mutual respect, and shared values. These types of relationships are long-lasting and provide real value over time.

Here are some key principles for building authentic connections and partnerships:

1. **Focus on Giving First**: One of the most effective ways to build strong relationships is by offering value to others.

Instead of approaching relationships with a mindset of "What can I get?" think about "What can I give?" Whether it's offering advice, providing a useful connection, or lending a helping hand, people are more likely to invest in a relationship when they see that you genuinely care about their success.

2. **Be Genuine and Transparent**: Authenticity is the foundation of any strong relationship. Be open, honest, and true to yourself in your interactions. People can sense when you're being insincere or trying to manipulate a connection for personal gain. Authenticity fosters trust, which is essential for building meaningful, long-term relationships.
3. **Show Interest in Others**: Relationships are built on mutual interest and understanding. Take the time to learn about the people you're connecting with—their goals, values, and challenges. Ask thoughtful questions and listen actively to their responses.

Showing genuine interest in others demonstrates that you value them as individuals, not just as a means to an end.

4. **Maintain Consistent Communication**: Building relationships requires effort and consistency. Stay in touch with people in your network regularly, whether through a quick message, a phone call, or an in-person meeting. Keep the lines of communication open and make time for nurturing the connections you've made.
5. **Look for Win-Win Opportunities**: Partnerships are most effective when both parties benefit. Look for ways to create win-win situations where you and your connections can mutually support each other's goals. When people see that collaborating with you brings value to both sides, they'll be more inclined to strengthen the relationship.
6. **Invest in Long-Term Relationships**: Relationships take time to develop. Be patient and willing to invest in the long term rather than seeking immediate rewards.

The most valuable connections are those that are nurtured over time, with trust and mutual support growing deeper as the relationship evolves.

## The Role of Mentorship and Giving Back

Mentorship plays a critical role in building relationships and achieving success. Whether you are seeking a mentor to guide you or becoming a mentor to help others, the exchange of knowledge and support in mentorship relationships accelerates growth for both parties.

1. **Finding the Right Mentor**: A good mentor is someone who has experience in areas you wish to grow in and is willing to invest in your development. To find the right mentor, look for individuals who align with your goals, values, and interests. Approach them with respect and express your desire to learn from their expertise. Mentors can offer valuable insights, challenge your thinking, and provide guidance during pivotal moments in your journey.

2. **Being a Mentor to Others**: As you progress in your own journey, becoming a mentor is a powerful way to give back and strengthen your network. Mentoring others not only allows you to share your knowledge and experience but also helps you develop leadership skills and deepen your understanding of your own path. By helping others succeed, you build a legacy of impact that enhances your own sense of accomplishment.
3. **The Importance of Giving Back**: Successful relationships are built on reciprocity, and giving back to others is an essential part of this dynamic. Whether it's mentoring, offering advice, or providing resources, giving back strengthens your network and fosters goodwill. When you invest in the success of others, they are more likely to support you in return. Moreover, giving back creates a sense of fulfillment and purpose, which enriches your journey toward success.
4. **Creating a Culture of Collaboration**:

One of the most effective ways to build a strong network is by fostering a culture of collaboration within your community or industry. Encourage partnerships, knowledge sharing, and mutual support among the people you connect with. When you cultivate an environment where people help each other succeed, everyone benefits from the collective success.

**Conclusion of Chapter 6**

Relationships are the true foundation of success, wealth, and power. The strength of your network determines the quality of opportunities, knowledge, and support available to you. By building authentic, long-lasting connections based on trust, mutual respect, and a commitment to giving back, you create a network that helps you achieve your goals and rise to new heights.

The role of mentorship, both as a mentee and mentor, is a crucial element in this journey. It accelerates growth, deepens relationships, and enriches the overall path to success.

Ultimately, valuing relationships is about more than just transactional exchanges; it's about investing in the people around you and creating a network that fosters collaboration, growth, and lasting success.

# Chapter 7: The Balance Factor – Mastering the Art of Life Harmony

In the pursuit of success, many people fall into the trap of focusing solely on one area of life—often their careers—while neglecting others. However, true success is not just about wealth, fame, or achievement. It's about living a balanced life where you can thrive in all areas: work, family, health, and personal growth. Finding balance is key to sustainable success, as it helps you maintain energy, avoid burnout, and enjoy a fulfilling life. In this chapter, we'll explore why balance is crucial for long-term success, strategies for juggling work, family, and personal growth, and how to avoid burnout while chasing your dreams.

## Why Balance Is Key to Sustainable Success

Many people believe that in order to succeed, they must sacrifice everything else in their life—personal time, family, hobbies, or health—for the sake of their career.

However, success that comes at the cost of your well-being or relationships is unsustainable. Without balance, burnout becomes inevitable, and your ability to enjoy your achievements diminishes.

Here's why balance is essential for long-term success:

1. **Maintaining Energy and Focus**: Balance ensures that you don't exhaust your physical, mental, or emotional energy in one area of life. By making time for rest, relationships, and personal development, you recharge and stay focused on your goals. People who maintain balance are more likely to sustain high levels of energy and productivity over time.
2. **Health and Well-Being**: A balanced life promotes better physical and mental health. Overworking without time for relaxation or self-care can lead to stress, anxiety, and health issues.

Prioritizing balance helps you stay healthy and resilient, which is necessary for achieving long-term success.

3. **Stronger Relationships**: Success is more enjoyable when you can share it with loved ones. By maintaining balance, you foster strong relationships with family and friends, ensuring that your support system remains intact. These relationships provide emotional stability and joy, contributing to your overall sense of fulfillment.
4. **Personal Fulfillment**: True success is not just about career achievements; it's about living a life that feels meaningful and rewarding. A balanced life allows you to pursue your passions, nurture your personal growth, and enjoy a variety of experiences. This holistic approach leads to greater happiness and fulfillment.
5. **Long-Term Sustainability**: Balance prevents burnout.

Many people experience short-term success by pushing themselves to the limit, but without balance, they eventually crash. A balanced approach allows you to pursue your dreams over the long haul, ensuring that your success is not fleeting but sustainable.

## Strategies for Balancing Work, Family, and Personal Growth

Achieving balance requires conscious effort and thoughtful planning. It's about setting priorities, managing your time effectively, and ensuring that all aspects of your life receive the attention they need. Here are some strategies for balancing work, family, and personal growth:

1. **Set Clear Priorities**: Balance starts with knowing what matters most to you. Take the time to identify your core values and priorities. For example, if family, health, and career are important to you, make sure that your schedule reflects those priorities.

Understanding your values helps you make decisions that support balance in your life.

2. **Create Boundaries Between Work and Personal Life**: One of the biggest challenges in maintaining balance is allowing work to bleed into personal time. Establishing boundaries is key. Set clear work hours and stick to them. Avoid checking emails or taking work calls during family time or personal activities. By creating boundaries, you ensure that each area of your life gets the attention it deserves.
3. **Use Time Management Techniques**: Time management is essential for balancing multiple responsibilities. Use tools like calendars, task lists, and time-blocking techniques to organize your day. Time-blocking involves scheduling specific blocks of time for different tasks—work, family, exercise, hobbies—so that each aspect of your life is accounted for. This helps you stay organized and ensures that you don't neglect important areas of your life.

4. **Delegate and Ask for Help**: You don't have to do everything on your own. Delegating tasks at work and asking for help from family or friends can lighten your load. Whether it's outsourcing tasks in your business, sharing household responsibilities, or seeking support from a mentor, don't be afraid to rely on others to help you manage your time effectively.
5. **Prioritize Quality Time Over Quantity**: When life gets busy, it's not always possible to spend large amounts of time in every area. Instead, focus on making the time you do have count. For example, even if you only have an hour with your family, make it quality time—be fully present, engage in meaningful conversations, and connect emotionally. The same goes for personal time; even short periods of self-care can have a big impact if they are intentional and focused.
6. **Schedule Time for Personal Growth**: Personal growth is often the first thing people sacrifice when life gets busy, but it's crucial for long-term success.

Make personal development a priority by scheduling time for activities like reading, learning new skills, or practicing mindfulness. Personal growth fuels your progress in other areas, keeping you motivated and inspired.

7. **Embrace Flexibility**: Life doesn't always go according to plan, and sometimes you'll need to adjust your schedule to accommodate unexpected events. Embrace flexibility as part of maintaining balance. It's okay to shift priorities temporarily when needed, as long as you return to your balanced routine once the situation stabilizes.

## Avoiding Burnout While Pursuing Your Dreams

Burnout is a common pitfall for those chasing ambitious goals, but it doesn't have to be inevitable. By adopting habits and practices that prioritize your well-being, you can stay energized and motivated on your path to success. Here are some strategies for avoiding burnout:

1. **Recognize the Signs of Burnout**: Burnout doesn't happen overnight—it's a gradual process that often starts with subtle signs like fatigue, irritability, and a lack of motivation. Recognizing these early warning signs is crucial for addressing burnout before it becomes overwhelming. Pay attention to how you feel, and take action if you notice signs of exhaustion or disengagement.
2. **Prioritize Self-Care**: Self-care isn't a luxury; it's a necessity for avoiding burnout. Make time for activities that rejuvenate your mind, body, and spirit. This might include regular exercise, meditation, spending time in nature, or engaging in hobbies you enjoy. Self-care helps you recharge and return to your goals with renewed energy.
3. **Take Breaks and Rest**: Pushing yourself to the limit without breaks leads to diminishing returns. Schedule regular breaks throughout your day to rest and reset. Additionally, make sure to take longer breaks—such as weekends or vacations—to fully disconnect and recharge.

Rest is essential for maintaining productivity and creativity in the long term.

4. **Practice Mindfulness and Stress Management**:
   Mindfulness practices like meditation, deep breathing, and journaling can help you manage stress and stay centered. Incorporating mindfulness into your daily routine helps you stay calm and focused, even when facing challenges. Stress management is key to maintaining balance and avoiding burnout.
5. **Set Realistic Expectations**:
   Ambition is important, but setting unrealistic expectations can lead to frustration and burnout. Break down your goals into smaller, achievable steps, and celebrate your progress along the way. Setting realistic expectations helps you stay motivated without overwhelming yourself with unattainable demands.
6. **Cultivate a Support System**:

Having a strong support system of friends, family, and mentors is essential for avoiding burnout. Surround yourself with people who encourage you, provide perspective, and offer help when needed. Sharing your challenges with others can provide relief and remind you that you're not alone in your journey.

7. **Align Your Work with Your Passions**: Burnout often happens when you're working on tasks that don't align with your passions or values. If possible, seek out work that excites and inspires you. When you're passionate about what you do, it's easier to maintain energy and motivation without feeling drained.

## Conclusion of Chapter 7

The balance factor is critical to long-term, sustainable success. By mastering the art of life harmony, you not only achieve your professional goals but also enjoy personal fulfillment, strong relationships, and good health. Balance allows you to pursue your dreams while staying energized and engaged in all aspects of your life.

Achieving balance requires setting clear priorities, managing your time effectively, and practicing self-care. It's about embracing flexibility, asking for help when needed, and making personal growth a priority. Most importantly, balance ensures that you don't burn out on the path to success, allowing you to enjoy the fruits of your labor while maintaining a sense of well-being and purpose.

When you master the art of balance, you create a life that's not only successful but also deeply satisfying.

# Chapter 8: Patience – The Virtue that Guarantees Success

In a world that thrives on instant gratification, patience is often overlooked as a critical component of success. Yet, the ability to wait, persevere, and stay focused through challenges and delays is a hallmark of those who achieve long-lasting success. Whether it's building wealth, gaining power, or achieving personal goals, the road to success is rarely a straight line. Patience allows you to play the long game, endure setbacks, and remain committed to your vision. In this chapter, we'll explore why patience is key to wealth and power, how to stay focused despite delays, and the importance of celebrating small wins along the way.

## The Long Game: Why Patience is a Key to Wealth and Power

Many people mistake success for something that happens overnight, but in reality, most successful individuals and businesses take years, even decades, to reach their goals. Patience is the virtue that allows you to endure the waiting period between starting something and seeing the fruits of your labor. It helps you stay grounded, maintain perspective, and continue moving forward, even when immediate results are not apparent.

Here's why patience is essential for wealth, power, and success:

1. **Compounding Effects Over Time**: Success often relies on small, consistent efforts over a long period. Whether it's investing in financial markets or building a career, the principle of compounding plays a huge role. Patience allows you to reap the rewards of cumulative growth—whether it's compound interest in investments or incremental progress in your personal and professional life. Wealth and power come to those who are willing to wait and build steadily over time.

2. **Resilience in the Face of Setbacks**: Success is never a smooth ride; there will be setbacks, delays, and failures along the way. Patience provides the mental fortitude to push through these obstacles without losing sight of your goals. It helps you to see setbacks as temporary roadblocks rather than insurmountable failures, giving you the strength to keep moving forward.
3. **The Ability to Make Thoughtful Decisions**: Patience encourages strategic thinking and careful decision-making. Those who rush into decisions often miss important details or overlook potential risks. In contrast, patient individuals take the time to gather information, weigh their options, and make informed choices. This thoughtful approach often leads to better outcomes, whether in business, relationships, or personal growth.
4. **Long-Term Relationships and Trust**: Building trust and meaningful relationships also requires patience. Whether you're developing a business partnership, cultivating a friendship, or nurturing a romantic relationship, trust grows over time.

Patience allows you to invest in these relationships, knowing that the long-term rewards—both personally and professionally—will be worth the wait.

## How to Stay Focused and Committed Despite Delays

One of the biggest challenges with patience is maintaining focus and commitment when progress seems slow or non-existent. Delays can be frustrating, and it's easy to feel discouraged when results don't come as quickly as you'd hoped. However, there are practical strategies that can help you stay the course and remain committed to your long-term goals.

1. **Keep Your Eyes on the Bigger Picture**: When progress slows down or you hit a roadblock, it's important to remind yourself of the larger vision. Take time to revisit your long-term goals and reflect on why you started in the first place. Keeping the bigger picture in mind can help you maintain perspective and stay focused, even when short-term results aren't visible.

2. **Break Goals into Smaller Steps**: Large goals can feel overwhelming, especially when they take years to achieve. One way to maintain momentum is by breaking your bigger goals into smaller, manageable steps. Each small victory will give you a sense of accomplishment and help you stay motivated. By focusing on the process rather than the outcome, you remain engaged and can appreciate the incremental progress you make along the way.
3. **Develop a Routine of Consistent Action**: Success is built on consistent effort. Create a daily or weekly routine that aligns with your long-term goals. Whether it's dedicating an hour each day to learning a new skill, working on your business, or saving money, consistency is key. Over time, these small, regular actions will lead to significant progress, helping you stay committed during periods of slow growth.
4. **Learn to Embrace Delays**: Delays and challenges are inevitable, but they don't have to derail your progress.

Instead of seeing delays as failures, view them as opportunities for learning or improvement. Often, a delay gives you the time to refine your approach, gather more information, or reassess your strategy. Embrace the delays as part of the journey, knowing that they can make you stronger and more prepared for future success.

5. **Stay Connected to Your "Why"**: Your "why" is the reason you're pursuing your goals in the first place. When frustration or impatience sets in, reconnecting with your purpose can help reignite your passion and commitment. Take time to reflect on what motivates you, whether it's providing for your family, achieving personal fulfillment, or making a positive impact on others. Staying connected to your purpose helps you push through the waiting period and remain committed.

# Celebrating Small Wins While Waiting for the Big Breakthrough

One of the secrets to maintaining patience is learning to celebrate small wins along the way. These small victories not only boost your motivation but also remind you that progress is happening, even if it's slower than expected. Celebrating small wins helps you stay positive and focused while waiting for the big breakthrough.

1. **Acknowledge Your Progress**: It's easy to get so focused on the ultimate goal that you overlook the progress you've already made. Take time to acknowledge and celebrate the steps you've taken, no matter how small. Whether it's completing a task, reaching a mini milestone, or learning something new, these achievements are part of your journey to success.
2. **Reward Yourself Along the Way**: Positive reinforcement can be a powerful motivator. Set small rewards for yourself when you achieve milestones.

These rewards don't have to be extravagant—perhaps it's a nice dinner, a weekend off, or simply taking time to relax and reflect on how far you've come. Rewarding yourself makes the process of waiting more enjoyable and reminds you that success is a series of steps, not a single moment.

3. **Track Your Achievements**: Keeping a journal or log of your progress can help you visualize how far you've come. Documenting your achievements, no matter how minor, gives you a tangible reminder of your growth. On days when you feel impatient or discouraged, looking back at your progress can provide a much-needed boost of motivation.
4. **Share Your Wins with Others**: Celebrating small wins is even more enjoyable when you share them with others. Whether it's a trusted friend, family member, or mentor, sharing your progress allows you to receive encouragement and support. It also helps reinforce the significance of the steps you're taking toward your ultimate goal.

5. **Appreciate the Journey, Not Just the Destination**:
   Success is not just about reaching the final goal; it's about the person you become along the way. Patience allows you to appreciate the journey—every lesson, every challenge, and every small victory that shapes your growth. By focusing on the process rather than just the outcome, you find fulfillment and joy in the steps leading to success.

**Conclusion of Chapter 8**

Patience is more than just a virtue—it is a powerful tool that guarantees long-term success. In a fast-paced world where instant results are often expected, those who master the art of patience gain an advantage. They understand that wealth, power, and personal success take time, and they are willing to invest in the long game.

By staying focused, maintaining commitment despite delays, and celebrating small wins, you create a mindset of perseverance that ensures you stay on track.

Patience allows you to endure the inevitable setbacks and challenges, and it provides the resilience needed to achieve your dreams. Remember, success is not just about the destination—it's about the journey and the growth that happens along the way.

With patience, you are better equipped to navigate the road to wealth and power, knowing that true success is built over time, one step at a time.

# Chapter 9: Belief in Yourself: The Core of Unstoppable Success

Belief in oneself is the foundation of every achievement. It's the driving force behind the pursuit of dreams, the courage to take risks, and the resilience to overcome setbacks. Without self-confidence, even the best-laid plans can falter. In this chapter, we will explore why self-belief is critical to achieving success, techniques to boost your self-esteem and inner strength, and strategies for overcoming self-doubt and imposter syndrome. Whether you're striving for wealth, power, or personal fulfillment, belief in yourself is the key that unlocks unstoppable success.

## The Importance of Self-Confidence in Achieving Success

Self-confidence is often the invisible asset that separates successful individuals from those who fall short of their potential.

It empowers you to take bold actions, seize opportunities, and persist in the face of challenges. Here's why self-confidence plays such a vital role in achieving success:

1. **Empowering Decision-Making**: Confidence allows you to trust your own judgment and make decisions without constant second-guessing. When you believe in yourself, you're more likely to take calculated risks, embrace new opportunities, and act decisively. This forward momentum is critical for progress, whether in your career, relationships, or personal life.
2. **Building Resilience**: Challenges and setbacks are inevitable on the path to success, but self-confidence equips you with the resilience to keep going. When you believe in your abilities, you can recover from failure more quickly because you know it doesn't define you. Instead, you see obstacles as opportunities for growth and learning.
3. **Attracting Opportunities**: Confidence is magnetic.

People are naturally drawn to those who exude self-assurance because they convey a sense of competence and leadership. When you believe in yourself, others are more likely to believe in you too—whether it's potential employers, business partners, or personal relationships. This attracts opportunities and opens doors to success.

4. **Breaking Through Comfort Zones**: Self-confidence is essential for pushing past your comfort zone. It gives you the courage to venture into the unknown, try new things, and take risks that others might shy away from. This is often where the biggest breakthroughs happen, and without confidence, you may miss out on these transformative experiences.
5. **Achieving Peak Performance**: Confidence enhances your ability to perform at your best. When you believe in your skills and capabilities, you can approach challenges with a clear mind, free from the crippling effects of doubt and fear. This enables you to tap into your full potential and deliver your best work.

# Techniques to Boost Your Self-Esteem and Inner Strength

While some people seem to be born with natural confidence, self-belief is a skill that anyone can cultivate. It requires practice, self-awareness, and intentional actions to build. Here are practical techniques for boosting your self-esteem and inner strength:

1. **Affirmations and Positive Self-Talk**: Your internal dialogue plays a significant role in shaping your self-confidence. Positive affirmations—repeated statements that reinforce your belief in yourself—can help shift negative thought patterns and boost your self-esteem. For example, saying "I am capable of achieving my goals" or "I am deserving of success" regularly can gradually reshape your mindset. The more you tell yourself something positive, the more your brain will begin to accept it as truth.
2. **Celebrate Your Achievements**:

It's easy to focus on what you haven't accomplished, but acknowledging your successes—no matter how small—builds confidence. Make it a habit to celebrate your wins, whether it's completing a challenging project, learning a new skill, or taking a step toward your goals. Reflecting on your achievements reminds you of your capabilities and reinforces your belief in your potential.

3. **Surround Yourself with Positive Influences**:
   The people around you have a profound impact on your self-esteem. Surround yourself with individuals who encourage, support, and believe in you. Seek out mentors, friends, and colleagues who lift you up and provide constructive feedback. Avoid toxic relationships that drain your energy or make you doubt yourself.
4. **Visualize Success**:
   Visualization is a powerful tool for building confidence. Spend time each day imagining yourself achieving your goals.

Picture the steps you'll take, the obstacles you'll overcome, and the success you'll enjoy as a result of your efforts. This mental rehearsal helps solidify your belief in your ability to succeed and prepares your mind for taking action.

5. **Practice Self-Compassion**: Being kind to yourself is crucial for maintaining self-confidence. Understand that everyone makes mistakes and encounters setbacks—it's a natural part of the journey. Instead of beating yourself up when things go wrong, practice self-compassion. Acknowledge your efforts, learn from your experiences, and move forward without harsh self-criticism.
6. **Challenge Your Comfort Zone Regularly**: Growth happens when you stretch beyond what feels comfortable. Make it a habit to step outside your comfort zone, whether that means speaking up in meetings, taking on new responsibilities, or pursuing opportunities that feel intimidating. Each time you face and overcome a challenge, your confidence grows.

# How to Overcome Self-Doubt and Imposter Syndrome

Even the most successful people experience self-doubt and imposter syndrome at times—the feeling that you're not as capable or deserving as others think you are. However, learning to overcome these feelings is essential for sustaining long-term success. Here are strategies to help you defeat self-doubt and imposter syndrome:

1. **Recognize Self-Doubt as Normal**: First, understand that self-doubt is a common human experience, especially when facing new challenges. It doesn't mean you're incapable or unworthy—it simply means you're stepping into uncharted territory. Acknowledging this helps you avoid over-identifying with self-doubt and prevents it from stopping you in your tracks.
2. **Keep a Success Journal**: Imposter syndrome often stems from a skewed perception of your accomplishments.

Keeping a journal of your successes, skills, and positive feedback from others can serve as a reminder of your capabilities. Whenever self-doubt arises, revisit your journal to reinforce your belief in yourself.

3. **Focus on Effort Over Perfection**: Perfectionism is often a root cause of imposter syndrome. Instead of striving for perfection, focus on giving your best effort. Accept that mistakes and imperfections are part of the process and don't define your worth. This shift in mindset helps alleviate the pressure to meet unrealistic expectations.
4. **Reframe Negative Thoughts**: When self-doubt creeps in, challenge those thoughts with facts and evidence. For example, if you think, "I'm not good enough to succeed," ask yourself, "What proof do I have to support this?" Then counter the negative thought with positive truths, such as "I have the skills and experience needed for this role" or "I've overcome challenges in the past, and I can do it again."

5. **Seek Feedback and Support**: Imposter syndrome can make you feel isolated, but seeking feedback from trusted mentors, peers, or coaches can provide reassurance. Often, others can see your strengths and potential more clearly than you can. Having supportive people in your corner helps to affirm your abilities and combat feelings of inadequacy.
6. **Take Action Despite Doubt**: The best way to overcome self-doubt is to take action, even when you feel unsure. Confidence grows with experience, so the more you face challenges head-on, the more you'll prove to yourself that you're capable. Each step forward chips away at self-doubt and reinforces your self-belief.

## Conclusion of Chapter 9

Belief in yourself is the cornerstone of unstoppable success. It fuels your ability to take risks, embrace opportunities, and persevere through challenges. By cultivating self-confidence, practicing positive self-talk, and pushing through self-doubt, you can unlock your full potential.

Success begins in the mind. When you believe in your capabilities, the world opens up with possibilities. You're no longer held back by fear, doubt, or uncertainty. Instead, you become the architect of your own destiny, confidently navigating the path to wealth, power, and fulfillment. Remember, the most important investment you can make is in your belief in yourself—because once you trust in your own abilities, nothing can stop you from achieving greatness.

# Chapter 10: Conclusion – Mastering the Habits of Success

Success is not a product of chance or luck. It's the result of deliberate choices, disciplined habits, and a mindset geared toward growth and perseverance. The habits we've explored throughout this book—embracing failure, crafting a clear vision, being a lifelong learner, mastering the art of listening, taking proactive steps, valuing relationships, maintaining balance, cultivating patience, and believing in yourself—are the building blocks that lead to sustained wealth, fame, power, and success. Now, as we reach the conclusion of this journey, let's explore how these habits interconnect, the roadmap to achieve your goals, and the key to sustaining success over the long term.

## Putting It All Together: How These Habits Interconnect

The nine habits outlined in this book are not isolated practices.

They are deeply interconnected and reinforce one another, creating a powerful framework for success. When you master one habit, it strengthens the others, creating a synergy that accelerates your growth. Let's briefly revisit how these habits work together:

1. **Embracing Failure** prepares you for the inevitable challenges of pursuing your vision. Without the fear of failure, you're more willing to take risks, which are essential for achieving big goals.
2. **A Clear Vision** gives you the direction needed to focus your efforts. It allows you to set meaningful goals that guide your proactive behavior and daily actions.
3. **Lifelong Learning** ensures that you stay adaptable in a constantly changing world. The more you learn, the more equipped you are to anticipate opportunities and proactively navigate challenges.
4. **Listening** strengthens relationships, both personally and professionally.

Effective listening helps you build connections, which in turn opens doors to new opportunities and partnerships.

5. **Proactivity** is the habit that keeps you moving forward. Instead of waiting for success to come to you, proactivity ensures you're consistently taking steps toward your goals, adjusting your approach as necessary.
6. **Valuing Relationships** amplifies your success through collaboration and mentorship. A strong network enhances your ability to achieve your vision, and giving back to others creates a cycle of support and growth.
7. **Balance** is critical for longevity. It ensures that while you're striving for success, you're also nurturing your health, relationships, and well-being, avoiding burnout and sustaining motivation over the long haul.
8. **Patience** enables you to stay committed during slow periods of growth. It teaches you to focus on steady progress and celebrate small wins, knowing that success is often the result of cumulative effort.

9. **Belief in Yourself** ties everything together. Without self-confidence, it's impossible to embrace failure, pursue your vision, or take proactive steps. Self-belief gives you the courage to keep moving forward despite setbacks, knowing that success is within reach.

Each habit reinforces the others, creating a virtuous cycle of growth and achievement. As you work to integrate these habits into your daily life, you'll find that they naturally strengthen one another, propelling you toward success at a faster pace.

## Your Roadmap to Wealth, Fame, and Power

Now that you understand the habits that lead to success, how do you turn this knowledge into a practical roadmap for achieving wealth, fame, and power? Here are the key steps to follow:

1. **Define Your Vision**: Clearly articulate what success looks like for you.

Is it financial independence, recognition in your industry, or influence over a particular field? The clearer your vision, the more focused your efforts will be.

2. **Set Specific, Actionable Goals**: Break down your vision into smaller, measurable goals. Each goal should be specific, time-bound, and aligned with your larger aspirations. This ensures that you're consistently working toward tangible outcomes.
3. **Embrace Failure and Learn from It**: As you pursue your goals, expect setbacks. Rather than seeing them as failures, view them as learning opportunities. Reflect on what went wrong, adjust your strategy, and move forward with renewed confidence.
4. **Continuously Learn and Adapt**: Stay committed to learning. Whether through formal education, self-study, or mentorship, make it a habit to constantly acquire new knowledge and skills that will keep you competitive and adaptable.

5. **Nurture Relationships and Build Your Network**:
Success is not achieved in isolation. Invest time in building authentic relationships with others. Seek out mentors, collaborate with peers, and offer your support to others. The more you give, the more you'll receive in return.
6. **Maintain Balance**:
Success should not come at the expense of your health, relationships, or personal well-being. Make time for self-care, family, and personal growth. Balance is essential for long-term sustainability.
7. **Stay Patient and Focused**:
Great success often takes time. Stay committed to your goals, even when progress feels slow. Celebrate your small wins along the way and keep your focus on the bigger picture.
8. **Act with Confidence**:
Trust in your abilities and take bold actions.

The more confident you are in yourself, the more likely you are to seize opportunities, overcome challenges, and achieve your goals.

## Sustaining Success Over the Long Term

Achieving success is one thing, but sustaining it over the long term requires ongoing effort and vigilance. Here are key principles to help you maintain success once you've achieved it:

1. **Keep Evolving**: The world is constantly changing, and so should you. Stay adaptable by continuing to learn and grow. Whether it's new skills, emerging trends, or shifts in your industry, stay ahead by evolving with the times.
2. **Never Stop Building Relationships**: Your network is one of your greatest assets. Continue to nurture your relationships and give back to those who have helped you along the way. Mentoring others and offering support will not only solidify your success but also help you leave a lasting legacy.

3. **Maintain Humility**: Success can sometimes breed arrogance, but humility is key to staying grounded. Remember that there is always more to learn, and no one achieves success alone. Stay open to feedback and maintain a growth mindset.
4. **Revisit and Refine Your Vision**: As you grow and achieve success, your goals may evolve. Periodically revisit your vision and make adjustments to reflect your current priorities. This ensures that you continue moving in the direction that aligns with your values and long-term aspirations.
5. **Practice Gratitude**: Gratitude keeps you focused on the positive aspects of your journey. Regularly acknowledging what you've achieved and appreciating those who have helped you along the way fosters a sense of fulfillment, making success more meaningful.
6. **Avoid Complacency**: Success can lead to comfort, but complacency is the enemy of growth.

Continue to challenge yourself, set new goals, and push beyond your current achievements. Staying hungry for growth ensures that your success remains sustainable.

**Conclusion of Chapter 10**

The habits outlined in this book are not quick fixes or shortcuts to success. They are long-term practices that require dedication, persistence, and a mindset geared toward growth. By mastering these habits, you can create a powerful foundation for wealth, fame, and power, and—most importantly—you can sustain your success over the long term.

Remember, the path to success is a marathon, not a sprint. There will be ups and downs, but with the right habits in place, you'll be equipped to navigate challenges, seize opportunities, and achieve the life you've always dreamed of. Keep embracing failure, learning from every experience, nurturing relationships, and believing in yourself.

Success is not just a destination—it's a journey, and with these habits, you're well on your way to mastering it.

# Chapter 11: Appendix – Resources for Personal Growth

Achieving long-term success requires continuous learning, self-reflection, and consistent action. To support your growth beyond this book, this appendix offers a selection of valuable resources—books, podcasts, courses, journaling prompts, and tools—to keep you on track and help you refine the habits necessary for wealth, fame, and power. These resources will provide deeper insights into personal development, mindset mastery, and practical skills for achieving your goals.

**Recommended Books, Podcasts, and Courses**

**Books**

1. **"Atomic Habits" by James Clear**
   A practical guide to building good habits and breaking bad ones, James Clear's book is perfect for anyone looking to understand how small, consistent actions lead to life-changing results. It's a must-read for mastering habit formation and long-term growth.

2. **"The Power of Now" by Eckhart Tolle**
   A guide to mindfulness and living in the present moment, this book helps readers cultivate patience, balance, and mental clarity, which are critical for achieving and sustaining success.
3. **"Mindset: The New Psychology of Success" by Carol S. Dweck**
   This book dives deep into the concept of a growth mindset, emphasizing that intelligence and talent are not fixed traits but can be developed through effort and learning—a key principle for lifelong growth.
4. **"Dare to Lead" by Brené Brown**
   Focused on leadership, vulnerability, and courage, this book is a powerful resource for anyone looking to improve their listening skills, build authentic relationships, and lead with empathy.
5. **"Grit: The Power of Passion and Perseverance" by Angela Duckworth**
   Angela Duckworth's research on grit highlights why passion and perseverance are key ingredients to success.

This book reinforces the value of patience, resilience, and sustained effort over the long haul.

**Podcasts**

1. **"The Tim Ferriss Show"** Tim Ferriss interviews top performers across various industries, uncovering their habits, routines, and mindsets for success. The podcast covers everything from productivity hacks to deep reflections on failure and self-belief.
2. **"The Tony Robbins Podcast"** Tony Robbins shares insights on personal development, business strategies, and achieving lasting success. With a focus on mindset, relationships, and proactive strategies, his podcast is a great resource for those looking to elevate their lives.
3. **"On Purpose with Jay Shetty"** Jay Shetty discusses how to cultivate purpose, mindfulness, and balance. He interviews thought leaders and shares personal stories that inspire growth in relationships, careers, and personal development.

4. **"The School of Greatness" by Lewis Howes**
   Focused on mastering the mindset of greatness, this podcast features interviews with successful individuals who share their personal journeys, failures, and strategies for overcoming obstacles and staying motivated.
5. **"How I Built This" by Guy Raz**
   This NPR podcast dives into the stories of entrepreneurs and innovators, focusing on how they built their empires from the ground up. It's an excellent source of inspiration and practical advice for taking proactive steps in your career or business.

## Courses

1. **"Personal Development Masterclass" on Udemy**
   This comprehensive course covers everything from goal setting and time management to mindset mastery and habit formation. It's a great all-in-one resource for personal growth.

2. **"Learning How to Learn" on Coursera**
   Based on neuroscience and cognitive psychology, this course provides techniques to help you learn faster and retain more information—crucial for lifelong learners.
3. **"The Science of Well-Being" by Yale University on Coursera**
   This free course focuses on building happiness and well-being through scientifically proven strategies. It's ideal for anyone looking to enhance their mindset, balance, and overall sense of fulfillment.
4. **"Effective Communication: Writing, Design, and Presentation" on edX**
   Offered by RIT, this course is essential for those looking to improve their listening and communication skills. It's particularly helpful for leaders and professionals seeking to build authentic relationships.
5. **"Building Relationships That Last" on LinkedIn Learning**

This course offers actionable tips for developing and maintaining meaningful personal and professional relationships, emphasizing the importance of empathy, trust, and effective communication.

## Journaling Prompts for Self-Reflection

Journaling is a powerful tool for personal growth and self-awareness. By regularly reflecting on your thoughts, goals, and actions, you can track your progress, gain clarity, and reinforce positive habits. Here are some journaling prompts to help you stay focused on your journey to success:

1. **What is one recent failure, and what did I learn from it?** Reflect on how you handled a setback, and identify the lesson it taught you. This will help you embrace failure and see it as an opportunity for growth.
2. **What is my vision for the next year, and how does it align with my long-term goals?** Write about your current vision and how it connects with your ultimate aspirations.

This prompt will help you clarify your direction and stay focused.

3. **How have I demonstrated a growth mindset recently?**
Think about a time when you embraced a challenge, learned something new, or stepped outside your comfort zone. This will reinforce your commitment to lifelong learning.

4. **How well am I listening to the people around me?**
Reflect on a recent conversation where you practiced active listening. How did it impact your relationships or understanding of the other person's perspective?

5. **What opportunities can I proactively pursue right now?**
Identify areas in your life where you can take control and initiate action. This prompt encourages you to be forward-thinking and seize opportunities.

6. **Who in my life am I grateful for, and how can I strengthen that relationship?**

Reflect on the people who have supported you and think of ways to show appreciation and nurture those connections.

7. **What areas of my life need more balance?**
Consider whether you are neglecting any aspects of your life—whether personal or professional—and write about strategies to restore balance.
8. **What small wins have I experienced recently, and how can I celebrate them?**
Acknowledge your achievements, no matter how small, and recognize the progress you've made. Celebrating wins keeps you motivated during the long journey to success.
9. **How am I cultivating patience in my personal or professional life?**
Write about situations that require patience and how you are practicing delayed gratification or long-term commitment.
10. **What limiting beliefs do I need to overcome, and how can I build self-confidence?**
Reflect on any doubts or fears that are holding you back.

Identify ways to replace those limiting beliefs with positive affirmations or actions.

## Tools for Tracking Progress on Your Journey

To stay consistent and accountable, it's important to track your progress. Here are some tools that can help you stay organized, measure your growth, and reinforce positive habits:

1. **Habit Tracker Apps (e.g., Habitica, Streaks, or Loop)**
   These apps allow you to set daily habits and track your progress over time. They provide reminders and visual cues to help you stay consistent.
2. **Goal-Setting Apps (e.g., Goals on Track or Strides)**
   Goal-setting apps are perfect for breaking down long-term aspirations into manageable milestones. You can set specific goals, track your progress, and celebrate your achievements along the way.

3. **Journaling Apps (e.g., Day One or Journey)**
Digital journaling apps help you reflect on your thoughts, record insights, and track your personal growth. They often come with prompts, reminders, and options to include multimedia elements.
4. **Mind Mapping Tools (e.g., MindMeister or XMind)**
Use mind mapping tools to visualize your ideas, organize your thoughts, and strategize how to achieve your goals. This is especially helpful for clarifying your vision and setting priorities.
5. **Time Management Tools (e.g., Trello, Todoist, or Asana)**
These project management tools help you stay on top of your daily tasks, long-term projects, and personal goals. They provide a structured way to organize your time and track progress.
6. **Gratitude Apps (e.g., Gratitude Journal or 5 Minute Journal)**

Practicing gratitude is a powerful way to stay positive and motivated. These apps encourage you to reflect on what you're thankful for each day, helping you maintain a success-oriented mindset.

7. **Mentorship Platforms (e.g., MentorcliQ or PushFar)**
Connecting with mentors can accelerate your success. These platforms help you find mentors in your industry, schedule meetings, and track your progress in the relationship.

## Conclusion of Chapter 11

Success is a lifelong journey, and these resources are tools to guide you along the way. By continuing to learn, reflect, and take consistent action, you'll stay aligned with the habits of wealth, fame, power, and personal fulfillment. Remember, the key to growth is not just the destination—it's embracing the journey, learning from every step, and consistently striving to be the best version of yourself.

www.ingramcontent.com/pod-product-compliance
Lightning Source LLC
Chambersburg PA
CBHW050311230526
45471CB00005B/2128